EXPLORING OPPOSITES

Before and After

by Joy Frisch-Schmoll

Consulting Editor: Gail Saunders-Smith, PhD

CAPSTONE PRESS
a capstone imprint

Pebble Plus is published by Capstone Press,
1710 Roe Crest Drive, North Mankato, Minnesota 56003.
www.capstonepub.com

Library of Congress Cataloging-in-Publication Data
Frisch, Joy.
  Before and after / by Joy Frisch-Schmoll.
    p. cm. — (Pebble plus. Exploring opposites.)
  Includes index.
  Summary: "Full-color photographs and simple text introduce the concepts of before and after"—Provided by publisher.
  ISBN 978-1-62065-118-6 (library binding)
  ISBN 978-1-62065-895-6 (paperback)
  ISBN 978-1-4765-2122-0 (ebook PDF)
1. Picture puzzles—Juvenile literature. I. Title.

GV1507.P47F74 2013
793.73—dc23   2012033229

Editorial Credits
Jill Kalz, editor; Ted Williams, designer; Wanda Winch, media researcher; Jennifer Walker, production specialist

Photo Credits
Corbis: Sean Justice, 11; Digital Vision (Getty Images), 17; Dreamstime: Darak77, 7, Dreamstimedk, 21; iStockphoto Inc: Jacek Chabraszewski, 5; Shutterstock: Jonathan Pledger, 9, Josef Muellek, cover, Sirko Hartmann, 15, Zai Aragon, 19; Wikipedia: O484, 13

Note to Parents and Teachers

The Exploring Opposites set supports English language arts standards related to language development. This book describes and illustrates the concepts of before and after. The images support early readers in understanding the text. The repetition of words and phrases helps early readers learn new words. This book also introduces early readers to subject-specific vocabulary words, which are defined in the Glossary section. Early readers may need assistance to read some words and to use the Table of Contents, Glossary, Read More, Internet Sites, and Index sections of the book.

Printed in the United States of America in North Mankato, Minnesota.
092012   006933CGS13

Table of Contents

What They Mean

Who's riding before you?

"Before" means ahead of

or in front of another object.

"After" means behind.

Before and after are opposites.

What's Before?

Which letter comes first?

A comes before B.

B is before C.

C is before D.

The big elephant walks
at the front of the line.
It walks before
the smaller elephants.

The green engine rolls
into the train station.
The other train cars come
after it.

Before and After

It's a race across the snow!

The lead dog runs

before the other dogs.

The sled comes after.

A penguin dives
into the icy water.
The other penguins
dive in after it.

You Try It: Before or After?

The horse stands

_____ the buggy.

The buggy rolls

_____ the horse.

The mother duck

walks _____

her ducklings.

They come _____ her.

Glossary

buggy—a light cart pulled by one horse

duckling—a young duck

engine—a machine that pulls a train

object—anything that can be seen and touched; a thing

opposite—as different as possible

Read More

Alda, Arlene. *Hello, Good-bye.* Plattsburgh, N.Y.: Tundra Books, 2009.

Cleary, Brian P. *Straight and Curvy, Meek and Nervy: More About Antonyms.* Words Are CATegorical. Minneapolis: Millbrook Press, 2009.

Gravett, Emily. *Dogs.* New York: Simon & Schuster Books for Young Readers, 2009.

Internet Sites

FactHound offers a safe, fun way to find Internet sites related to this book. All of the sites on FactHound have been researched by our staff.

Here's all you do:

Visit *www.facthound.com*

Type in this code: 9781620651186

Check out projects, games and lots more at
www.capstonekids.com

Index

Word Count: 116
Grade: 1
Early-Intervention Level: 16